GET LOST!

A Travel Guide for Anywhere

Lee Crutchley

lost

VERB

    Past and past participle of *lose*.

ADJECTIVE

1   Unable to find one's way; not knowing one's whereabouts.

1.1 Unable to be found.

1.2 Unable to understand or to cope with a situation.

also by Lee Crutchley

The Nocturnal Journal

How to Be Happy (Or at Least Less Sad)

The Art of Getting Started

Quoteskine Volume 1

Get Lost!

A Travel Guide for Anywhere

LEE CRUTCHLEY

A TARCHERPERIGEE BOOK

tarcherperigee

An imprint of Penguin Random House LLC
penguinrandomhouse.com

TarcherPerigee with tp colophon is a registered trademark of
Penguin Random House LLC.

Most TarcherPerigee books are available at special quantity discounts for bulk purchase
for sales promotions, premiums, fund-raising, and educational needs. Special books or
book excerpts also can be created to fit specific needs. For details, write: Special
Markets@penguinrandomhouse.com.

ISBN 9780143130802

Printed in China
10 9 8 7 6 5 4 3 2 1

Designed by Lee Crutchley

for Jayne
there's no one I'd
rather get lost with

on getting lost

I feel like I should begin this book with an explanation of why it exists. So, the short answer is that I get lost, a lot, and I think you should too. I know that probably sounds stupid. How can you get lost when you have access to the whole world in your pocket? How can you get lost when you can walk down every street before you even leave home? How can you get lost *at* home?

Well, you have to get lost on purpose. You have to embrace getting lost as a state of mind, rather than a physical description, and you have to think of your smartphone as a safety net, rather than something you must follow blindly. Soon enough you will realize that getting lost has never been easier. It has also, in my opinion at least, never been more important.

Ten years ago, I quit my job, sold all of my possessions, and bought a ticket to travel the world. It felt like a crazy and terrifying (read: stupid) decision, but also like it could be one of the best decisions I would ever make—which, of course, it was. Over the year that followed I saw things I never imagined I would, and did things I never imagined I could. I also got lost, over and over again. I got lost physically, mentally, and metaphorically.

I was lost while playing crazy golf in a derelict theme park. I was lost while swimming with wild dolphins (after driving two hundred miles in the wrong direction). I was lost while waiting for my friends alone at the top of a mountain. I was still lost when a passing guide congratulated me for hiking up the most beautiful route, before informing me that it was also the old route, and my friends would be hours ahead by now.

As cliché as it sounds, each time I got lost I felt like I found a piece of myself—a piece I hadn't even realized was missing.

Some of my memories from that trip are cloudy these days. Especially the memories of everything I checked off the list of Things You *Must* Do Before You Die. I'm never sure if I'm remembering the experience itself, or just the photographs of it. Those memories feel like postcards now. Incredible and breathtaking images, albeit two-dimensional and flat.

But I still remember every detail of walking back down that mountain. Every tiny village, every smiling villager, every sound, and every smell—and I still remember Chitra, the young Nepali who walked with me for over an hour, showing me the way.

When I arrived back home in England, I turned down my old job and started to draw instead. I had no real plans for what would come next; drawing just felt right. I know how ridiculous that sounds, trust me. But ten years later, I have my dream job writing books and drawing pictures. Obviously traveling the world for a year was not a magical path leading to that dream job. There was a lot of hard work involved, and even more luck. But everything started with that first uncertain step.

I have since come to believe that the best moments on any trip, and in any life, are the moments less planned, the decisions less certain, and the roads less traveled. The moments when you have no expectations of what will happen, who you will meet, or where you will end up. Those are the moments you will remember forever, and those are the moments that will shape you—in ways you can't even begin to imagine.

I just looked up Chitra's name, to make sure I had the correct spelling, and I learned that Chitra means *drawing* or *picture*. Sometimes you have to get lost in order to find your way.

I am here

so are you

about this book

This is not the kind of guidebook that will tell you who serves the best latte or where the locals get sushi. It doesn't know where you are, where you have been, or where you are going. This book will probe you with questions, and send you on a journey to find answers. It can be used at the top of a mountain, on top of a bus, or in your own backyard. This book is a catalyst for curiosity.

It will never lead you down the beaten path, or even the less beaten one. It *will* lead you to more questions. This book will ask you to embrace uncertainty, until you are hooked on chasing it. It will force you to get lost, again and again, and it will help you to feel found. It will encourage you to choose your own adventure, and then live it. This book is one hundred beginnings, unlimited middles, and not a single end.

Following everyone else's adventures is boring—it's time to start creating your own. It's time to Get Lost!

how to use this book

1. flip to a random page.

2. answer the question on the right and follow the prompts.

3. #GetLost!

follow these directions
↑→↑→↑←↓←

Follow them until you feel ready to stop.

ARE YOU LIVING
OR EXISTING?

LIVING
GO TO PAGE 118

EXISTING
GO TO PAGE 196

go to the end of the line

Take a train as far as it goes.

HAVE YOU RESEARCHED
THIS PLACE?

YES
GO TO PAGE 88

NO
GO TO PAGE 72

eat the dessert special

If you're not sure what the local specialty is, ask someone. If there's more than one, eat them all.

HEAD OR HEART?

HEAD
GO TO PAGE 130

HEART
GO TO PAGE 36

follow
every
dog

Follow the first dog you see today. When you see another dog, switch and follow that one. Keep following each new dog until you feel ready to stop.

IS IT YOUR
FIRST DAY HERE?

YES

GO TO PAGE 88

NO

GO TO PAGE 60

let your senses guide you

Whether it's the smell of food or an interesting sound. Slow down, don't think too much, and follow whichever senses are pulling at you the most.

DO YOU BELIEVE IN
LOVE AT FIRST SIGHT?

YES

GO TO PAGE 128

NO

GO TO PAGE 172

find
each
other

Each go somewhere independently and try to find each other again. It's up to you whether you rely on your instincts, or send each other clues.

DO ALIENS EXIST?

YES
GO TO PAGE 24

NO
GO TO PAGE 106

bury some treasure

Draw a map to this treasure and leave it for a stranger to find.

DO YOU HAVE SWIMWEAR?

YES
GO TO PAGE 170

NO
GO TO PAGE 112

explore your room

Imagine your room is a city and explore every inch of it. Decide on the landmarks, post photos of the attractions, and share recommendations about this place.

TEACHING
OR LEARNING?

TEACHING
GO TO PAGE 178

LEARNING
GO TO PAGE 204

find the perfect souvenir

Find (don't buy) something to keep as a permanent reminder of this trip.

DO YOU
KEEP A DIARY?

YES
GO TO PAGE 172

NO
GO TO PAGE 114

follow
the
sunset

Let yourself be guided by the colors of sunset: orange, purple, red, and yellow. Gravitate toward these colors in everything you do and see today.

IS YOUR LOCATION
URBAN OR NATURAL?

URBAN
GO TO PAGE 146

NATURAL
GO TO PAGE 184

take
no
photos

Don't take a single photo all day, and don't look at Instagram or any old photos you've taken. Enjoy the day through your own eyes rather than a lens or screen.

ARE YOU STUCK
IN A RUT?

YES
GO TO PAGE 148

NO
GO TO PAGE 138

reverse your regrets

Think of your biggest regrets and spend the day finding ways to let go of or move on from them.

HAVE YOU TRIED
THE LOCAL CUISINE?

YES
GO TO PAGE 82

NO
GO TO PAGE 116

follow your lucky number

For example, if your lucky number is 7: walk in blocks of 7, only eat at places in building number 7, or take the number 7 bus and see where you end up.

DO YOU FEEL RUSHED?

YES
GO TO PAGE 118

NO
GO TO PAGE 160

eat
for
free

**Go to a food market and eat as
many free samples as you can.**

DO YOU HAVE
A KITCHEN?

YES
GO TO PAGE 82

NO
GO TO PAGE 192

spread some love

Write a message on every bank note you spend today.

DID YOU PACK
TOO MUCH?

YES

GO TO PAGE 76

NO

GO TO PAGE 28

hunt for treasure

Spend the day hunting for clues, and follow them until they lead you to treasure.

DO YOU FEEL
CONNECTED TO NATURE?

YES
GO TO PAGE 68

NO
GO TO PAGE 46

follow
the
river

**Find a river, or any other body of water,
and walk along the edge as far as you can.**

HOT OR COLD?

HOT
GO TO PAGE 170

COLD
GO TO PAGE 154

walk on the grass

Find the nearest patch of grass and walk on it barefoot for at least ten minutes.

ARE YOU IN
A FOREIGN COUNTRY?

YES
GO TO PAGE 124

NO
GO TO PAGE 152

wake up before the sun

Tomorrow morning, wake up before the sunrise and find a quiet spot to fully appreciate it.

DO YOU GET A
FREE BREAKFAST?

YES
GO TO PAGE 176

NO
GO TO PAGE 100

revisit favorite places

Spend the day visiting your favorite countries without leaving this one. For example: watch a martial arts movie, drink a Belgian beer, or take a salsa class.

DO YOU HAVE FOMO?
(FEAR OF MISSING OUT)

YES

GO TO PAGE 80

NO

GO TO PAGE 54

write your name in the streets

Plan a route that spells out the letters of your name on a map, then walk along it.

DO YOU HAVE
HEADPHONES?

YES
GO TO PAGE 134

NO
GO TO PAGE 120

snap every selfie

Every time you see someone taking a selfie today, take a photo of them taking that selfie.

WOULD YOU RATHER
BE SOMEWHERE ELSE?

YES
GO TO PAGE 174

NO
GO TO PAGE 182

be a micro tourist

Go back to your favorite tourist spot and choose a tiny detail. Examine this detail as if it were the most important thing in the city. Invent an elaborate story about this detail in case people ask you about it.

ARE YOU HERE WITH SOMEONE YOU LOVE?

YES
GO TO PAGE 22

NO
GO TO PAGE 114

sit
and
watch

Find a place to sit and people-watch. Imagine the stories behind the most interesting people you see. What do they do? Where are they going? Who do they love?

THE FUTURE
OR THE PAST?

THE FUTURE
GO TO PAGE 194

THE PAST
GO TO PAGE 204

make your own map

Create a map based on your experiences and leave it behind when you go home.

ARE YOU NATURALLY ADVENTUROUS?

YES

GO TO PAGE 136

NO

GO TO PAGE 180

visit
the
supermarket

Spend some time walking around grocery stores.
How do they differ from stores back home? What
do they tell you about the people who live here?

DO YOU HAVE A CAR?

YES
GO TO PAGE 174

NO
GO TO PAGE 14

go window shopping

Spend time looking at things you want, but don't need or can't afford. Why do you want them so much, and what things do you actually need that you don't have?

ARE YOU LONELY?

YES
GO TO PAGE 178

NO
GO TO PAGE 142

stay
up
late

Go for a walk, or look out of the window. What's happening in any rooms that are illuminated? Where are the cars heading? Why are other people awake?

QUESTIONS
OR ANSWERS?

QUESTIONS
GO TO PAGE 104

ANSWERS
GO TO PAGE 126

eat
locally
grown

**Eat some locally grown fruit and
find somewhere to plant the seeds.**

ARE YOU MOTIVATED MORE BY POSITIVES OR NEGATIVES?

POSITIVES
GO TO PAGE 142

NEGATIVES
GO TO PAGE 190

go
on a
date

Pick a local date spot and have a romantic evening there. If you're alone, date yourself for the night.

DO YOU LIKE SHOPPING?

YES
GO TO PAGE 64

NO
GO TO PAGE 28

be more social

Look at hashtags relating to your location and use them as your guide for the day. Imagine each post is a recommendation given directly to you.

DREAMS OR REALITY?

DREAMS
GO TO PAGE 58

REALITY
GO TO PAGE 200

follow
the
clouds

Let yourself be guided by clouds. Follow the direction
they move or point. If there are no clouds, which way
would you go if you were a cloud?

ARE YOU AN
ANIMAL LOVER?

YES

GO TO PAGE 18

NO

GO TO PAGE 162

give away what you don't need

Fill a bag with things you don't need. Take a walk and distribute them as you go: give them away, donate them to charity, or sell them. Keep walking until they're all gone.

DO YOU FEEL
LIKE A TOURIST?

YES

GO TO PAGE 92

NO

GO TO PAGE 166

use the wrong guide

Find a guide for a different place and use it as a guide for this one. Eat in restaurants with the same names, find similar landmarks, and seek out the same hidden gems.

OUTSIDE OR INSIDE?

OUTSIDE
GO TO PAGE 18

INSIDE
GO TO PAGE 26

wait
in
line

Every time you see a line today, join it and wait until you get to the front. Do you want what they are offering?

DO YOU FEEL
TOO SAFE?

YES
GO TO PAGE 198

NO
GO TO PAGE 208

cook like a local

Invent your own twist on a famous local dish.

HAVE YOU SEEN ALL THE MUST-SEE SIGHTS?

YES

GO TO PAGE 180

NO

GO TO PAGE 202

get
off
early

On each journey you take, get off the train or bus at
least three stops early and walk the rest of the way.

DO YOU HAVE A MAP?

YES
GO TO PAGE 162

NO
GO TO PAGE 12

be
guided
by color

**Let this color guide you today. Walk
toward it, turn every time you see it,
let it pull you in any way that feels right.**

ARE YOU NEAR
THE OCEAN?

YES

GO TO PAGE 102

NO

GO TO PAGE 164

talk
to
strangers

Ask a stranger to recommend an area and go there.
In that area, ask someone to recommend a street,
then ask someone on that street their favorite thing
to do. Do that thing, and keep following this cycle
of recommendations for the whole day.

CAN YOU SPEAK
THE LANGUAGE?

YES
GO TO PAGE 210

NO
GO TO PAGE 62

walk the alphabet

Find the first and last streets alphabetically
and travel (ideally walk) between them.

DO YOU FEEL
AT HOME?

YES
GO TO PAGE 152

NO
GO TO PAGE 168

go the wrong way

Plan the direct route to get everywhere you want to go today, then deliberately avoid that route.

ARE YOU BORED?

YES
GO TO PAGE 52

NO
GO TO PAGE 32

build
a
fort

Build a fort using whatever you can find in your room.

DO YOU HAVE ENOUGH
TIME TO SEE EVERYTHING?

YES
GO TO PAGE 190

NO
GO TO PAGE 160

always do the opposite

Whatever your guidebook, people, or the internet recommends for you today, do the opposite.

ARE YOU IN A
24-HOUR CITY?

YES
GO TO PAGE 108

NO
GO TO PAGE 36

leave some postcards

Write some postcards and leave them in places for strangers to find.

DO YOU FEEL INSIGNIFICANT?

YES
GO TO PAGE 106

NO
GO TO PAGE 66

eat breakfast for dinner

Breakfast for dinner is always a good idea.

IS IT RAINING?

YES
GO TO PAGE 94

NO
GO TO PAGE 112

look
at the
ocean

**Spend at least ten minutes looking at
the ocean. Imagine someone beyond
the horizon looking directly back at you.
Imagine what you would say to each other.**

DO YOU HAVE
A FAVORITE SONG?

YES
GO TO PAGE 120

NO
GO TO PAGE 124

flip
a
coin

Every time you are faced with a choice today, flip a coin to make the decision for you. There is no best of three, or five. Go with the result of the first flip.

ARE YOU FEELING LOST?

YES
GO TO PAGE 12

NO
GO TO PAGE 84

gaze
at the
stars

Find the darkest place you can tonight, and look at the stars.

DO YOU USE INSTAGRAM?

YES
GO TO PAGE 156

NO
GO TO PAGE 202

be a nocturnal tourist

Visit your favorite tourist spots tonight, and see how different they are after dark.

$1 OR $1,000?

$1
GO TO PAGE 140

$1,000
GO TO PAGE 64

try
new
things

For the whole day, try only new things.
Walk a new route, eat foods you've
never tried, or say hello to strangers.

ARE YOU IN LOVE?

YES
GO TO PAGE 70

NO
GO TO PAGE 128

build
a
boat

Build some kind of boat or raft, as big or as small as you like, and find a place to sail it.

DO YOU
BELIEVE IN GOD?

YES
GO TO PAGE 74

NO
GO TO PAGE 186

write
a love
letter

Write a love letter to someone you don't know.
It can be a stranger you've passed or someone
you've only imagined. Leave the letter in a
place you think that person will find it.

ARE YOU HUNGRY?

YES
GO TO PAGE 122

NO
GO TO PAGE 40

eat
like
a local

Eat as many local delicacies as you can find (or as many as you can stomach).

DO YOU FEEL ENERGETIC?

YES
GO TO PAGE 148

NO
GO TO PAGE 102

stand absolutely still

Go to the busiest spot in town and
stand absolutely still for a few minutes.

HAVE YOU BEEN HERE BEFORE?

YES

GO TO PAGE 96

NO

GO TO PAGE 158

imagine your song

Imagine your favorite song is playing as the soundtrack to everything you do today.

ARE YOU TRAVELING FOR MORE THAN 14 DAYS?

YES

GO TO PAGE 42

NO

GO TO PAGE 48

eat
three
courses

Get each course from a completely different place.

DO YOU HAVE
A FAVORITE COLOR?

YES
GO TO PAGE 86

NO
GO TO PAGE 44

find
new
favorites

Spend the day trying to find a new favorite song, food, place, person, etc....

ARE YOU ALONE?

YES
GO TO PAGE 166

NO
GO TO PAGE 22

teach someone a lesson

Send a postcard about the things you've learned on this trip.

DO YOU HAVE
A PEN AND PAPER?

YES

GO TO PAGE 144

NO

GO TO PAGE 52

fall in love, over and over

Make a mental note of every person that you could easily fall in love with today.

ARE YOU HAPPY?

YES
GO TO PAGE 138

NO
GO TO PAGE 192

trust your instincts

Follow your urges without questioning your desires or stopping to think about whether something is a good idea. Just go with it, whatever it is (unless it puts you in danger).

DO YOU HAVE
A GUIDEBOOK?

YES

GO TO PAGE 90

NO

GO TO PAGE 78

take people's selfies

Every time you see someone taking a selfie today, offer to take a photo of them instead.

ARE YOU IN
A GOOD PLACE?

YES
GO TO PAGE 20

NO
GO TO PAGE 134

play your song

Play your favorite song and walk until it's finished. Change direction and do the same again. Keep doing this until you end up where you're supposed to be.

DO YOU FEEL LUCKY?

YES
GO TO PAGE 80

NO
GO TO PAGE 140

always
say
yes

**Every time you are asked a question today,
say yes (as long as it doesn't put you in danger).**

HAVE YOU CHANGED
TIME ZONES?

YES

GO TO PAGE 46

NO

GO TO PAGE 146

send
some
love

Send a postcard to someone you love.

DO YOU BELIEVE
IN YOURSELF?

YES
GO TO PAGE 92

NO
GO TO PAGE 130

make a wish, or ten

Gather any small coins you have.
Find as many fountains as you can,
and make a different wish in each.

ARE YOU SHY?

YES

GO TO PAGE 132

NO

GO TO PAGE 210

142

go
with
the flow

Follow the general flow of people for the whole day.

ARE YOU ADDICTED
TO YOUR PHONE?

YES
GO TO PAGE 20

NO
GO TO PAGE 72

tell the world one thing

Write one thing you want to tell the world on as many scraps of paper as you can find. Leave these notes inside copies of your favorite books in different bookstores.

OPTIMISM OR PESSIMISM?

OPTIMISM
GO TO PAGE 38

PESSIMISM
GO TO PAGE 206

cross every bridge

Cross as many bridges as you can today. If there are no real bridges, cross metaphorical bridges instead.

DO YOU HAVE A LIST OF MUST-SEE ATTRACTIONS?

YES
GO TO PAGE 200

NO
GO TO PAGE 26

reach
the
top

Find the highest point you can and get to the top.

ARE YOU RUNNING AWAY FROM SOMETHING?

YES
GO TO PAGE 198
NO
GO TO PAGE 96

fulfill your purpose

Spend the day doing things that you feel you're meant to do with your life.

SWEET OR SALTY?

SWEET
GO TO PAGE 16

SALTY
GO TO PAGE 38

pretend you're not here

Imagine you are somewhere else, and live today as if you were there instead.

ARE YOU READY
FOR ANYTHING?

YES
GO TO PAGE 136

NO
GO TO PAGE 182

pay
it
forward

Next time you buy a drink, get two. Take a walk
while you drink one, and give the other to the
first person who looks like they need it.

DO YOU THINK
ABOUT OTHERS MORE
THAN YOURSELF?

YES
GO TO PAGE 150

NO
GO TO PAGE 40

be someone else

Look at the social media posts tagged at every place you visit today. Re-create one photo in each different spot.

NIGHT OR DAY?

NIGHT
GO TO PAGE 108

DAY
GO TO PAGE 62

find what you're looking for

Make a list of people, places, or things you hope to find on this trip. Start actively looking for them today.

DO YOU GET ANXIOUS?

YES
GO TO PAGE 58

NO
GO TO PAGE 34

see
it
all

Take a whirlwind tour of all the must-see attractions, allowing time for only one photo at each of them. Try to see everything on your list.

ARE YOU A FUSSY EATER?

YES
GO TO PAGE 100

NO
GO TO PAGE 116

explore your favorite shape

Draw your favorite shape over a map of your location. This is your boundary for the day. Explore the very edges of this shape, but always stay inside of it.

DO YOU FEEL BRAVE?

YES
GO TO PAGE 184

NO
GO TO PAGE 94

study great art

Choose something that you think deserves to be a famous work of art, and study it as if it were.

DO YOU TAKE TOO MANY PHOTOS?

YES

GO TO PAGE 32

NO

GO TO PAGE 56

pose with something you love

Ask people to take a photo of you with
your favorite thing every time you see it.

ARE YOU AN INDEPENDENT PERSON?

YES
GO TO PAGE 110

NO
GO TO PAGE 74

visit your alternate home

Find the street that has the name closest to the street where you live. Go there and pretend you've just left your house for the day.

BOOKS OR MOVIES?

BOOKS
GO TO PAGE 144

MOVIES
GO TO PAGE 54

take
a
dip

Find the nearest body of water and stand in it (puddles count). If there is no water nearby, stand in the bathtub or shower.

COULD YOU LIVE HERE?

YES
GO TO PAGE 60

NO
GO TO PAGE 16

never
forget
them

Write a diary entry about a stranger
that you don't want to forget.

HAVE YOU LEARNED ANYTHING ABOUT YOURSELF ON THIS TRIP?

YES
GO TO PAGE 126

NO
GO TO PAGE 132

head
up
north

Travel north until you reach the
third neighborhood or town.

SUNRISE OR SUNSET?

SUNRISE
GO TO PAGE 48

SUNSET
GO TO PAGE 30

feed someone in need

Give your next meal away.

ARE YOU HOMESICK?

YES
GO TO PAGE 168

NO
GO TO PAGE 206

spread
the
word

Send a group email about the interesting
things you've learned about this place.

HEAVY OR LIGHT?

HEAVY
GO TO PAGE 208

LIGHT
GO TO PAGE 200

be less of a tourist

Find less popular alternatives to the biggest tourist spots today. For example, start at the main cathedral and walk away from it until you find a tiny church.

DO YOU HAVE PURPOSE IN LIFE?

YES
GO TO PAGE 150

NO
GO TO PAGE 188

take
a
staycation

Draw a one-mile square around your accommodation.
Explore this area in as much detail as possible.

HAVE YOU EATEN?

YES
GO TO PAGE 176

NO
GO TO PAGE 122

climb the tallest tree

Find the tallest tree and climb as high as you can.

NIGHT OUT OR NIGHT IN?

OUT
GO TO PAGE 70

IN
GO TO PAGE 66

go
to
church

Go to a church or other religious building. Sit quietly for a while and think about the reasons why people have faith. Who or what do you truly believe in?

HAVE YOU SEEN
THE GOONIES?

YES
GO TO PAGE 42

NO
GO TO PAGE 24

buy only local products

Only buy things that are made or grown as close to your location as possible today.

DO YOU TRAVEL OFTEN?

YES
GO TO PAGE 50

NO
GO TO PAGE 158

test
your
brain

Choose a place you really want to visit tomorrow, and look at it on a map. Wake up and go there using only your memory and instincts (no maps or phones allowed).

ARE YOU HAVING FUN?

YES
GO TO PAGE 98

NO
GO TO PAGE 110

eat your favorite

Eat your favorite type of food for every meal today, including snacks.

HAVE YOU BEEN USING PUBLIC TRANSPORTATION?

YES
GO TO PAGE 84

NO
GO TO PAGE 14

be who you want to be

What would you do if there was nothing stopping you? What kind of person would you be if you never doubted yourself? Be that person for the whole day.

DO YOU HAVE REGRETS?

YES

GO TO PAGE 34

NO

GO TO PAGE 50

do what you love

List your three favorite things to do and spend at least one hour enjoying each of them today.

NATURAL OR MAN-MADE?

NATURAL
GO TO PAGE 30

MAN-MADE
GO TO PAGE 56

face your fears

Confront your biggest fears today, in the smallest ways.

ARE YOU ADDICTED
TO SOCIAL MEDIA?

YES
GO TO PAGE 98

NO
GO TO PAGE 156

~~don't~~

look

down

**Take a photo of your feet at every
point of interest you visit today.**

DO YOU FEEL READY?

YES
GO TO PAGE 194

NO
GO TO PAGE 104

spot
the
tourists

Completely ignore every attraction you visit today, and look only at the other tourists.

RED OR BLUE?

RED
GO TO PAGE 86

BLUE
GO TO PAGE 44

learn in the lobby

Go into the lobby of every museum or gallery you pass. What can you learn from these lobbies alone?

ARE YOU TOO
MATERIALISTIC?

YES
GO TO PAGE 76

NO
GO TO PAGE 188

head toward home

Follow anything that reminds you of home today.

IS IT CLOSER TO SUMMER OR WINTER?

SUMMER
GO TO PAGE 68

WINTER
GO TO PAGE 154

go as high as you can

**Find the tallest building and ride
the elevator as high as you can.**

WORK OR PLEASURE?

WORK
GO TO PAGE 164

PLEASURE
GO TO PAGE 196

ask
more
questions

Think of one big question you have about life.
Ask everyone you meet today that question.

IS THIS TRIP
HARD OR EASY?

HARD
GO TO PAGE 90

EASY
GO TO PAGE 78

things I don't want to forget...

OBERBAUMBRÜCKE

things I don't want to forget...

GANSBAAI

things I don't want to forget...

things I don't want to forget...

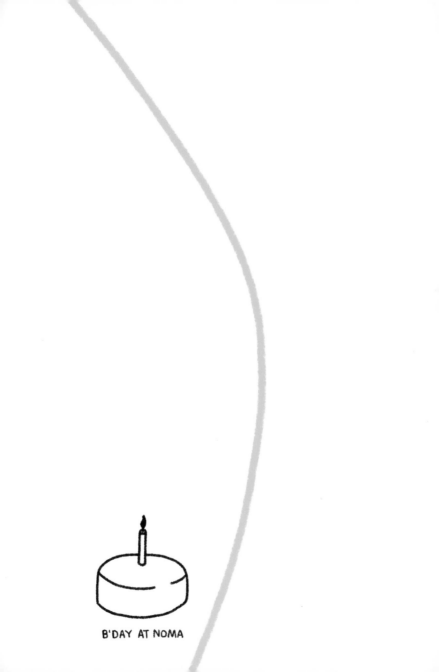

B'DAY AT NOMA

all that

does not

not all th

wander

is gold

glitter,

ose who

are lost.

—J.R.R. Tolkien

thanks to...

Jayne: for putting a blue ribbon on my brain.

Teresa: for saying "You should come too."

Laurie Abkemeier: for being Laurie Abkemeier.

My mom: for . . . well, everything. But specifically, for supporting my decision to start drawing and see what happens.

Marian Lizzi: for continuing to believe in my ideas.

And The Goonies: never say die.

© Jayne Yong

Lee Crutchley is a writer and artist based in Berlin, Germany (although he is probably somewhere else as you read this). His previous books include *The Nocturnal Journal* and *How to Be Happy (Or at Least Less Sad)*.

He wrote *this* book while surrounded by elephants in South Africa, ice fishing on a frozen lake in Norway, snorkeling the turquoise oceans of the Seychelles, eating lemon-flavored ants in Denmark, eye to eye with great white sharks in Gansbaai, walking for miles through the snowy streets of Berlin, and in many other places both near and far.

His most treasured possession is his passport.

found

Past and past participle of *find*.

Having been discovered by chance
or unexpectedly.